Top Notes

T0360055

Amanda Lohrey's

Vertigo

Study notes for Standard English:
Module A
2015-2020 HSC

Bruce Pattinson

—— A ——
FIVE SENSES
PUBLICATION

Five Senses Education Pty Ltd
2/195 Prospect Highway
Seven Hills 2147
New South Wales
Australia

Pattinson, Bruce,
Top Notes – Vertigo
ISBN 978-1-76032-017-1

CONTENTS

Introduction To The Top Notes Series iv

The Standard Course 1

Experience Through Language 3

Related Texts 8

Summary 9

Studying A Fiction Text 10

Language Techniques 11

The Composer 12

Putting The Novella In Context 14

Plot Summary 17

Questions 29

Setting 33

Character Analysis...36

Thematic Concerns 42

Language 49

Model Essay 53

The Essay...54

Model Essay Outline – *Vertigo* 56

Distinctively Visual: Other Related Texts 58

Other Responses To Practise 67

INTRODUCTION TO THE TOP NOTES SERIES

Top Notes are designed with the high school student in mind. They are written in an easy to read manner yet discuss the important ideas and issues that you need to understand so you can successfully undertake your English HSC examinations.

They are written by practising teachers who have years of experience and contain many helpful tips for the course and examination. They focus specifically on the student's needs and examine each text in the context of the module it has been allocated to.

Each text includes:

- Notes on the specific module
- Plot summary
- Character analysis
- Setting
- Thematic concerns
- Language studies
- Essay questions and a modelled response
- Other textual material
- Study practice questions
- Useful quotes

I am sure you will find these Top Notes useful in your studies of English.

Bruce Pattinson
Series Editor

THE STANDARD COURSE

This is a brief analysis of the Standard course to ensure you are completely familiar with what you are attempting in the examination. If in any doubt at all, check with your teacher or the Board of Studies.

The Standard Course requires you to have studied:

- Four prescribed texts. This means four texts from the list given to your teacher by the Board of Studies.

- For each of the texts, one must come from each of the following four categories.
  - drama
  - poetry
  - prose fiction (novel usually)
  - nonfiction or media or film or multimedia texts. (Multimedia are CD-ROMs, websites, etc.)

A range of related texts of your own choosing. These are part of your Area of Study, Module A and Module C. Do not confuse these with the main set text you are studying and focusing on. This is very important. The set text should be the major focus in extended responses with about sixty percent of content dedicated to discussion of core text material and forty percent on related material.

Paper One

Area of Study: Discovery

Paper Two

Module A	Module B	Module C
Experience through Language	**Close Study of Text**	**Texts and Society**
Electives	• Drama	*Electives*
• Distinctive Voices	OR	• Exploring Interactions
OR	• Prose Fiction	OR
• Distinctively Visual	OR	• Exploring Transitions
	• Nonfiction, Film, Media, Multimedia	
	OR	
	• Poetry	

You must study the Area of Study and EACH of Modules A, B and C

There are options within EACH of these that your school will select.

EXPERIENCE THROUGH LANGUAGE

ELECTIVE TWO : Distinctively Visual

The Experience Through Language module requires you to always have language as the focus of your study and, therefore, your response. The syllabus states that you should be focusing on how language can shape and change our perceptions of other people throughout the world. It also focuses on how the use of language can alter our relationships with others. The Board says about this Module,

'This module requires students to explore the uses of a particular aspect of language. It develops students' awareness of language and helps them understand how our perceptions of and relationships with others and the world are shaped in written, spoken and visual language.' (p11.)

You will be studying a specific text, in this case *Vertigo* by Amanda Lohrey. In your responses, you should always be discussing how language has been used as a technique by the composer.

The elective that you will be studying in this module is called, "Distinctly Visual". Read how the Board interprets this Elective,

'In their responding and composing, students explore the ways the images we see and/or visuals in texts are created. Students consider how the forms, features and language of different texts create these images, affect interpretation and shape meaning. Students examine one prescribed text, in addition to other related texts of their own choosing that provide examples of the distinctively visual.' (p12)

In other words you will be studying how visual images are used to shape meaning or how written words create visual images. Now many students are a little confused at first since they are often reading words on a page and not looking at pictures. They ask, "How can I look at the visual?" You need to see this elective as the exploration of visual images. All composers try and encourage the audience to see images in their mind as they experience the text. For many years you have studied imagery in novels and poetry and never thought to ask for a photo! You will be exploring and analysing how composers use visual images to send messages or portray meaning to the audience. Composers often send messages or emphasise certain aspects of a character, a relationship, an event or an idea through the use of visual images. Visual, narrative and poetic techniques are often employed by composers to create such images through language and art.

An example might help. Visual images are usually clear in films, posters and pictures. They may still be clear in written texts, but may not be as literally visual. For example, the composer of a graphic may have put a love heart between two people to indicate that they felt love for each other or were falling in love. Another example is in cartoons where the audience can see the heart of a character beating (often in a love heart shape) in their chest as the person they love walks by. Usually this is simply emphasising, through a visual symbol, the emotion that the composer wants you to notice. You may pick up the message that the character is in love simply by their body language facing the character, touching the other person frequently or even simply their facial expressions.

Thus, the composer has already portrayed their idea to us without the character even having to say, the word "love". Similarly, we get messages or get meaning from the descriptions of a character's body language. When they are not verbalising anything, we are still picking up meaning from actions. An actor may be saying the words, "I hate him" and we are also reading in the narrative about their body language, facial expressions and other techniques to confirm this or, perhaps, deny this if it is said sarcastically. These things emphasise the character's feelings for that person.

In this way, the messages the audience "read" through visual cues are just as important as what the actor is saying in helping us build visual images about the text. In some cases, as suggested there may be inconsistencies in what a character is actually saying and the way he/she is described as acting. This is very important for the audience to know and is consequently why it is so important that we can all read visual images and not just focus on the spoken language of a text.

Other visual aspects to a text may be thematic. This means the composer may create visual images to promote ideas.

Here techniques such as imagery are very useful. A composer might use a technique like symbolism to help represent a message they would like the audience to think about. Other composers might add more meaning to a particular object by having it take on a symbolic significance. (For example, a motif - is a reoccurring symbol and may convey meaning due to an added significance, linked to its connotation.)

Now that you are more advanced in your study of English, the techniques are a little subtler. As you should already know, the visual images we get from description 'talk' to us and give us messages as discussed above. It is your job to explore what the main messages are in a text and then investigate how the artistic and linguistic cues present visual images which convey messages.

Visual aspects that are used to give the audience clues about that character and are often seen in visual texts such as films, include the clothing (costume), the style (hair and makeup), the setting and the way all of these things have been put together, the mise en scene. All indicate something about the character. A messy bedroom will emphasise to the audience that this character is in a chaotic time in their life or that they are a lazy person who is not interested in looking after themselves. These aspects can be conveyed through a lens or through another artistic medium or through words.

When you consider how relationships are represented you will find that the composer can use many techniques to show how people interact. The types of imagery used are always carefully chosen. An uneasy relationship may be associated with unpleasant or violent images or symbols.

The ideas of a text are considered very important and these are often emphasised through distinctive images. If a writer wanted to celebrate a particular place you would expect the images created to be positive. Perhaps the images are vibrant and exciting, full of bright colours and attractive images and people. You job would be to examine how the visual images have been crafted to represent the composer's ideas (to make meaning). It is also important you consider how different composers do this in different ways. Be ready to compare and contrast. It is important to see how effective composers have been. This is why you will also be asked to gather related texts that you choose yourself. This elective requires you to become an expert on how a variety of composers such as authors, poets, film directors and artists create and use the distinctively visual, not just Lohrey.

You are urged to revise the language of imagery as well as the language and vocabulary of visual literacy. Techniques will be an important aspect of this module titled, Experience through Language and of this elective, titled Distinctively Visual.

RELATED TEXTS

This module expects you to look at other texts and see how the distinctively visual has been used by composers to shape meaning. You will probably chose to gather some related texts that are essentially 'viewed' (unlike your prescribed short stories which are written texts) Think for instance about film, paintings photographs and many advertisements. It is a good idea to explore differing text type as it is important you show that you understand that a range of texts create visual images in different ways. You have been studying images in your junior years and should be familiar with many common terms associated with visual literacy. These will be very useful when you come to discuss a visual related text. You should be familiar with words such as salience, vectors, foregrounding reading paths, perspectives, gaze, the colour palette, framing and size.

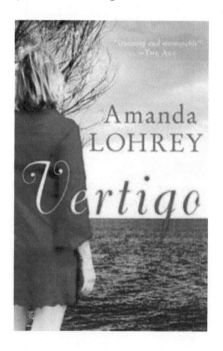

SUMMARY

Techniques like:

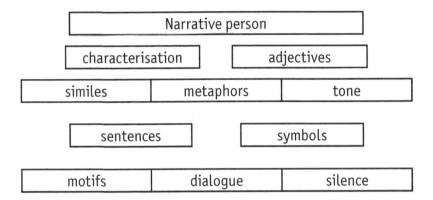

Narrative person		
characterisation		adjectives
similes	metaphors	tone
sentences		symbols
motifs	dialogue	silence

can make distinctive visual images

to shape meaning & to shape audience response

can make responders

more engaged, entertained and persuaded to believe a message immersed in a text

STUDYING A FICTION TEXT

The medium of any text is very important. If a text is a novel this must not be forgotten. Novels are *read*. This means you can refer to the "reader" but the "responder" is the preferred term when you are referring to the audience of any text.

The marker will want to know you are aware of the text as a novel and that you have considered its effect as a written text.

Remembering a fiction text is a written text also means when you are exploring *how* the composer represents his/her ideas you MUST discuss language techniques. This applies to any response you do using a novel, irrespective of the form the response is required to be in.

Language techniques are all the devices the author uses to represent his or her ideas. They are the elements of a fiction that are manipulated by authors to make any novel represent its ideas effectively! You might also see them referred to as stylistic devices or narrative techniques.

Every fiction uses techniques differently. Some authors have their own favourite techniques that they are known for. Others use a variety to make their text achieve its purpose.

Some common narrative techniques are shown on the diagram that follows.

NARRATIVE TECHNIQUES

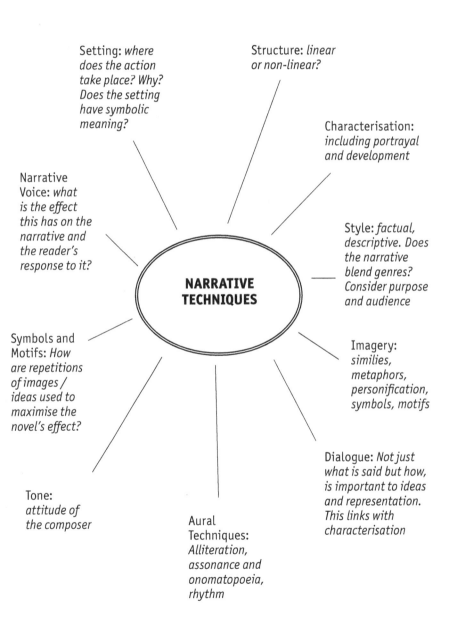

Setting: *where does the action take place? Why? Does the setting have symbolic meaning?*

Structure: *linear or non-linear?*

Characterisation: *including portrayal and development*

Narrative Voice: *what is the effect this has on the narrative and the reader's response to it?*

Style: *factual, descriptive. Does the narrative blend genres? Consider purpose and audience*

NARRATIVE TECHNIQUES

Symbols and Motifs: *How are repetitions of images / ideas used to maximise the novel's effect?*

Imagery: *similies, metaphors, personification, symbols, motifs*

Tone: *attitude of the composer*

Dialogue: *Not just what is said but how, is important to ideas and representation. This links with characterisation*

Aural Techniques: *Alliteration, assonance and onomatopoeia, rhythm*

THE COMPOSER

Amanda Lohrey-Writer (1947-)

"I'm trying to capture a sense of the numinous, a sense of being a small part of a great whole, that wonderful feeling that has nothing to do with God or religion."

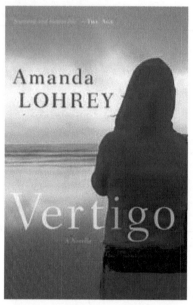

Amanda Frances Lillian Lohrey (1947-) is an Australian author who now works out of the University of Queensland. As well as being a novelist she also pens essays. Some of her essays may be found at http://www.themonthly.com.au/author/amanda-lohrey A more comprehensive analysis of her biographical details and works can be found at the following links.

The link below is to the official site of her publisher.

HTTP://WWW.BLACKINCBOOKS.COM/AUTHORS/AMANDA-LOHREY

The following is a lengthy article on Lohrey written by Geordie Williamson and published in The Australian newspaper. It discusses her work in general terms.

HTTP://WWW.THEAUSTRALIAN.COM.AU/ARTS/REVIEW/AMANDA-LOHREY-IS-A-CLASS-ACT/STORY-FN9N8GPH-1226597132344?NK=CAB4F7992D97A2C7128E24855FEBE807

The link below is to an Australian Broadcasting Commission site that explores Lohrey's work in terms of thematic concerns and her influences.

HTTP://WWW.ABC.NET.AU/RADIONATIONAL/PROGRAMS/BOOKSHOW/READING-MAD-AME-BOVARY-AN-INTERVIEW-WITH-AMANDA/2961178

Again the link below isn't specifically on *Vertigo* but it does give good background to her work and the ideas that drive Lohrey's writing. It includes some discussion on techniques.

HTTP://WWW.THEAGE.COM.AU/ARTICLES/2004/03/17/1079199287180.HTML?FROM=STORYRHS

PUTTING THE NOVELLA IN CONTEXT

Vertigo is an Australian novella but deals with universal concerns such as love. Thus, it has a wide appeal. Two other issues, that may cause some concern for readers, are the concepts of seachange/treechange which are dealt with in later sections of this study guide and bushfires which can be readily researched for those have no direct experience of such events. Most readers will have seen footage on television of bushfires and the problems they cause.

It is recommended that you read the two articles below which offer a deep insight into the construction and development of *Vertigo* and how Lohrey conceived and perceives the novella. These two links take you to pages directly relevant to your studies. Some of this information I have quoted in the body of this guide. Read the articles carefully, they are not long, and they will help you gain a clear insight into the text.

The first is an interview from the Age newspaper in Melbourne with Lohrey which covers her novella and its relevance and composition.

HTTP://WWW.THEAGE.COM.AU/NEWS/ENTERTAINMENT/BOOKS/THE-FIRE-OF-FIC-TION/2008/11/13/1226318837617.HTML

The second is an interview from Radio National which can be downloaded but I used the transcript which is accessible by clicking the relevant button on the page. It is an extensive interview on the text covering a wide range of issues. It is highly recommended.

HTTP://WWW.ABC.NET.AU/RADIONATIONAL/PROGRAMS/BOOKSHOW/AMANDA-LOHREYS-VERTIGO/3179466#TRANSCRIPT

PLOT OUTLINE

Luke is introduced

Anna is introduced

They decide to move to
the coast from the city

Their lives are in need
of change

Life in Garra Nalla is
good for Luke who is
bird-watching

A house is found in
Garra Nalla

Anna becomes unsettled
and misses 'the boy'

Gil is their neighbour
and he becomes a friend

Anna and Luke befriend
the Watts family

The first smoke from the
bushfire is seen in the
distance

Preparations are made
around the house as the
fire comes nearer

The wind continues and
the town is threatened

The fire arrives and
they are rescued then
evacuated

It is a cathartic moment
for both as 'the boy'
disappears and then
they seem to adjust

Luke and Anna return
and find the house is fine

The township returns to
some form of normality

Anna and Luke appear
to reconcile and are
ready to restart their
lives

PLOT SUMMARY

Vertigo, a pastoral novella is unusual in its structure as it is written in three extended sections rather than in a more regular structure, using chapters.

The adjective 'pastoral' also warrants analysis as this will enable us to get an idea of Lohrey's concept prior to engaging with the content of the narrative. Some definitions of a pastoral, from dictionary.com, are:

1. having the simplicity, charm, serenity, or other characteristics generally attributed to rural areas: *pastoral scenery; the pastoral life.*

2. pertaining to the country or to life in the country; rural; rustic.

3. portraying or suggesting idyllically the life of shepherds or of the country, as a work of literature, art, or music: *pastoral poetry; a pastoral symphony.*

4. a poem, play, or the like, dealing with the life of shepherds, commonly in a conventional or artificial manner, or with simple rural life generally; a bucolic.

These definitions all allude to the idyllic lifestyle that Luke and Anna are searching for when they leave the city behind to live in Garra Nalla. But what does it mean for our reading of the novel? In one sense it is the supposed relaxed and gentle atmosphere of the country that our two characters expect from their move. Yet it is also, in the context of our study, the images Lohrey creates to describe the supposed sleepiness of the town which makes the contrast with the fire so great. Later, we will examine the symbolism of the fire but for now let us begin to explore the narrative. Don't forget the impact of the graphics interwoven with the text. Think, as you read, about why they are there, how you see their effectiveness and what contribution they make to the text. You might also evaluate whether the images provided detract from the imaginative processes of the reader as we visualise the scene in our minds.

I

Lohrey's opens with a description of Luke Worley's newfound interest in bird watching. At the age thirty-four, since moving to the coast with his wife, Anna, he had taken up this new interest. The couple moved from the city for Anna's asthma where there were few birds and more pollution. With his own position under question he broaches the subject of moving to the country with Anna and she is 'receptive'. Work would go with them as they were independent in that regard and both felt a need to change with their youth fading and little hope of affording housing. Anna felt she needed something more than her current life and was in a 'spiritual impasse'.

They begin to plan their move and to search for locations with some conditions. Eventually they come across Garra Nalla which is a small place of about eighty houses. Garra Nalla is described in detail and is perfect for them. Later they find it has a dangerous beach and their friends say 'there's nothing here!' Yet the Federation era house was just right, especially when they found it was affordable. Luke wasn't concerned about the perils of rural living and so they moved in and began a new phase in their lives.

(Note, all through this search we get the image of the 'son' who is with them. This is a recurring image and later it is revealed he is the son they lost to a miscarriage - it is like an emotional link manifested that seems entirely real to them.)

Life changes pace for them and Anna has given Luke new binoculars so he can bird watch. They take much pleasure in identifying the Striated Pardalote and even more in the house which they adore. Even the 'boy' loves the verandah. The couple build a garden, live by the seasons and so begin to develop a rhythm similar to the earth's.

The only problem is the drought. Their tanks are low and some days water is the only topic. Gilbert Reilly (Gil) is their widower neighbour and he fills them in on local folklore and gossip and they also learn the idiosyncrasies of their other neighbour, Rodney Banfield, the local plumber who is having an affair and allegedly growing dope.

Luke begins to develop patterns of behaviour and prefers walking to swimming. He enjoys, and is often mesmerised by, the bird life. One day walking home, he sees a bird that is entirely new to him and he is 'elated'. He can't find the bird's name in his research but he tells Anna it is like their boy, who was never named. Luke then 'sees' "the boy" the next morning. We then read the story of the old squatter's mansion and how the new owners do not fit into the local scene. Gil has caught them shooting at swans, a once common occurrence.

Anna purchases a canoe despite having never paddled anything before but they soon learn after a lesson from local boy, Jacob. They glide across the water and begin to spend the evenings and sometimes the 'boy' is with them. Luke begins to dream around this time, mostly about "the boy". He reads at night when it's quiet while Anna trawls the cable news channels just as her father did. In the old shed out the back, Luke has found two trunks full of dusty books left by the old vicar. These books are not all theology but more travel writing which Luke gives himself over too. He reads *The Land That Is Desolate, a book of journeys in Palestine* and the author is very critical of the place. He stops reading and heads out to the verandah to engage with nature.

II

The couple are settling to life in the country. They now have to contend with the drought as they are on tank water. They also have to understand the weather. Luke finds he is more 'practical' than he has ever been before. Luke and Anna develop a friendship with Alan and Bette Watts who have two children, Zack and Briony. They play tennis together and one day, after meeting the helicopter pilots from the army base, Luke realises he is old before his time and regrets it. The topic turns to water and Alan has devised some water saving ideas and is thinking of buying a desalination plant. Anna tells Bette they have put starting a family on hold, hoping the 'boy' isn't listening.

Ken, Luke's father comes to stay. He is a 'restless' man, not yet adjusted to retirement. He thinks the place isn't suitable for a family and wonders why Luke isn't 'sick of it'. They linguistically dance around that 'other business' with Anna. Anna notices how Ken is unsettled and that "the boy" never appears when he or Gil are around.

Spring is now well underway. It appears to be a 'difficult' one as no rain has fallen and the winds are strong. It is the worst wind for many years and everything vegetative seems burnt and faded. Anna tries to maintain her routine of running and swimming but the wind, after forty-one days is getting on her nerves. Anna has her first encounter with a snake after the washing blows off the line and this, according to Gil, makes her a local. Months pass and the rains don't come. Here the weather is the 'plot' not the backdrop as it is in the city. Anna writes of it to her sister in Hong Kong. It is the topic of conversation and Anna is beginning to feel trapped, unlike Luke who can avoid it as a distraction.

While Anna might consider leaving, Luke won't even think about it yet. He has an overload of work which is interfering with his reading yet he manages to get to Jerusalem as he follows Sir Frederick Treves on his journey through Palestine. Treves reminds Luke of his father, rational and sceptical. Anna continues to watch the cable news and sees bloodied images of the Iraqi war. Anna is content that her 'boy' will not have to be a soldier. Alan and Luke talk about the travel books and the conversation turns to Gil's grandson in Afghanistan where he is a commando. Gil never talks about it because of superstition. Luke realises he hasn't thought about the 'boy' for a long time now. On the way home he sees a dead swan.

It is November. The air is dry and it gets hotter each day. Even the native animals are struggling. On the verandah in the evening Anna thinks about moving back to the city while Luke watches a sea eagle fly. She broaches the subject but he continues to watch the eagle. She goes inside and Luke is aware of her every move, he just doesn't know how to respond. 'Luke Worley is not a fool' and

Luke agrees to house sit for some friends in Randwick. As they leave Garra Nalla, Luke looks back and knows it's home.

When they arrive in the city he becomes 'irritable and censorious' and leaves after five days. Anna enjoys it more and loves escaping the wind but in the second week she misses her home. She feels she doesn't belong anywhere anymore but does notice "the boy" is missing in the city and thinks he sides with his father. Anna decides she needs a project and buys a book on coastal plants so she can leave a legacy in Garra Nalla when she leaves. Anna decides on she-oaks to begin her garden as she loves the way they have a 'eerie whistle' in the wind.

When she arrives back home Luke and Gil are getting materials to build a snake proof fence and Gil warns her against she-oaks as they 'burn like buggery'. Anna checks on this and finds he is correct. One night Gil comes over angry that a 'consortium' is going to take over sheep land for a tree farm that will surround the community. It threatens to increase the fire risk, wreck the water table and increase chemicals in the area. Anna is upset but Luke shrugs it off and again Anna thinks "the boy" takes his side.

As time passes Anna begins to resent Luke, feeling that her desire for him is not enough. She thinks he has lost ambition and the sharpness he had back in the city. She thinks he wastes time with Rodney, watching birds. He returns one day from his meandering walks and she thinks him a stranger. She has 'lost her roots' and feels disorientated, perhaps because "the boy" has gone and "the inner landscape of her consciousness is beginning to fade."

III

At the end of November Anna and Luke head to the nursery with the Watts. They then have lunch at the renovated Wolga pub. This makes Anna feel better and the following Sunday they plant their saplings according to Anna's plan and then have a celebration with Gil and the Watts. When the guests leave Luke takes Anna inside to make love after which they fall asleep. When they awake there is smoke in the air. It is a bushfire that is a long way away at that point. Alan Watts returns and says its a 'hell of a conflagration' and he reassures them no bushfire has ever reached the coast.

The next morning the smoke is in the house and covers the town but they can't see any flame. Anna checks her asthma medication which she hasn't used since living at Garra Nalla. The day is a scorcher and it's impossible to keep cool. The smoke gets worse and cuts visibility. The wind comes at night. They can now see the flames which are engrossing with their 'queer beauty'. They feel the tension now despite the distance of the fires and Anna realises she hasn't seen "the boy" for weeks which keeps her awake all night. At dawn she is consoled by the comfort of her kitchen before she returns to bed to sleep. Later she awakens to find Luke with tea and news that the fires are at the foothills. They now need to prepare for the fire which they do by completing jobs like gutter cleaning. Anna has soot all over her by the time she is finished. They then find the power cut and realise they have no pumps to defend the house.

They head to Gil's to see what's happening and he is barbecuing sausages. He says the fire has never reached the coast so they return home, have dinner and settle in for the night. Luke returns to Sir Frederick Treves' *Travels in Palestine* as the story 'haunts' him. Finally the author finds something that does not disappoint him, Damascus. Treves writes about it with 'lyrical descriptions' and Luke wonders how a Christian could be made 'happy' by a 'citadel of Islam'. While he reads, Anna works on her laptop writing to her sister in Hong Kong but she is content here and not jealous of her sister. Later she worries that the fire will come and wonders what they might lose. She dreams they have to leave but can't find "the boy" and she awakens to lighter winds. Luke, however, says things are getting worse and they are under full alert on the coast.

They listen to the radio as things worsen. Wolga and the pub have been destroyed and a second front has begun outside the town. Alan rings and they decide to play tennis to break the tension, staying by the sea rather than fleeing. As they play they see a Forestry chopper fly over and Luke notices Anna is using her puffer. They are exhausted by the heat and go home to shower and then walk to the headland to see the fire but as they can do nothing they head home to wait. In the afternoon the winds come and everything turns a 'dull greyish yellow'. The winds get worse, about one hundred and forty kilometres an hour and they decide to go back to the headland despite the wind. They can see this is where the townspeople have gathered and they can see the fire coming. Around the point they can see houses being eaten by the flames and even the sandhills burn.

Later the wind changes and the fire on the sandhills begins to turn on itself. They feel safer but Luke says he'll stay to watch as he wouldn't be able to sleep anyway. Suddenly Bette sees the fire from the north sweeping down which they hadn't seen because of the southern fire. The fire races at the town and breaks across the paddocks to the 'edge of the settlement'. Some are told to head to the rocks and sea while Anna and Luke go home to fight for their home. The house is well prepared and Luke heads outside as the fire strikes suddenly. Luke rushes back to the house to get Anna inside as the 'tidal wave of flame' hits them. Now they cannot escape to the water and as Luke prepares to go outside to fight a fire truck arrives and they get in. It instantly takes off as the flames surround it and they race away as the truck begins to melt around them. They make it to the lagoon under Luke's directions and the driver thinks they are very lucky.

The truck leaves and they then see many of the local people at and in the lagoon to escape the heat. Anna joins them and around her neck are her cds in a plastic bag. The plastic has melted and she thinks how stupid of her. Luke is very concerned about her and repeats 'Are you alright?' She replies she is. Darkness has now come but they can only hear the fire as the smoke is thick. Later they are taken across the lagoon where the police tell them they are to be taken to a church hall for the night. They are told they cannot return home as the town is a crime scene.

At the hall they meet survivors who have fared worse than they have. Anna finds an empty mattress while Luke gets food and drink. Luke half-heartedly eats then falls asleep and Anna fondly thinks this is typical of him. She cannot sleep and looks around the hall, dozing off until pain in her shoulder wakes her. She finds "the boy" snuggling into her and she traces his features with her finger. She knew he was 'indestructible'.

At dawn they 'stumble' out of the hall and all they can see are charcoal remains. Only three houses in Garra Nalla have been destroyed and they wonder whose they were. They learn their home has been untouched except for a 'thin layer of ash' over everything. They find a dead bird inside, it is the bird in the banksia tree and Luke is 'distraught', much to Anna's exasperation and anger. She moves to the bedroom to shower, which will make things better, when she sees his blue jumper on the bed. It has a brown scorch mark from where an ember came in through the broken pane. It didn't catch or the house may have burnt down. She wants to cry but saves it for later when Luke calls for her. He is on the verandah watching Gil rake embers. They move toward him and Luke shouts. Gil waves casually and they ask about the Watts. They are home and Gil is happy no one is dead.

They learn Garra Nalla had survived a 'perfect firestorm' and the Watts had survived by clinging to the rocks in the sea. Gil says he was terrified of losing his kids. Later that evening Luke slips away from the house and wanders through the nature reserve. It has been destroyed and he feels 'gutted'. He weeps and is back in the hospital where Anna had prematurely birthed "the boy". They had never suspected complications and in their shock had just thought of him as "the boy". They had scattered his ashes at sea. Luke wore the jumper that had saved them in the fire. At home Anna worries about Luke and has searched for him all over town but heads home. Here she talks disconnectedly to her mother and then cleans up. Luke returns late in the evening and she sees she has been crying. She has never seen him cry before and he says it isn't the fire and she knows it is "the boy". They hold each other for a long time and that night "the boy" comes in a dream to her. He waves to her and dissolves and she awakens crying until she lies staring into the dark.

On the third Sunday in December the townspeople gather on a windless day to celebrate their 'deliverance'. It is important for the kids to see things are normal and as the party winds up Anna is feeling a little drunk back at the Watts'. She now thinks she might go off the pill as life is so 'unpredictable' you shouldn't hold off decisions. She looks out over the lagoon and sees a figure, "the boy", heading out to a sloop, for his next destination. She now knows he is leaving them and she is at peace with the knowledge. Then Bette sees the swans have returned.

Luke sleeps when they arrive home because of his drinking at the party and is lost in a dream about birds. Anna takes time in the bathroom but isn't sleepy so she goes into the kitchen to watch the cable news. Not all the she-oaks were burnt and she thinks back to when Luke paddled her across the lagoon with "the boy" nestled in her arms. The final visual is the 'ghostly images' of the television in the dark.

QUESTIONS

Section One

1. Why do you think Lohrey begins *Vertigo* with Luke and his new bird watching habit? What impression is the composer making about him and the way he lives?

2. Anna is introduced next and Lohrey builds a picture of her and her life. How do you see Anna after this initial reading?

3. What motivates the Worleys to move to Garra Nalla?

4. Describe Garra Nalla in your own words.

5. What is it about the house that inspires them to buy it?

6. Give three examples of how Luke changes after the move.

7. Why does water become an obsession for them?

8. Describe Gil and state his impact on the couple.

9. How do you feel about the continual appearance of "the boy" in the novella? What impact on the narrative does he have? Should he be described as a character?

10. What happens in Luke's recurring dream?

11. Who was A.E. Henley Esq and what treasures has he left for Luke to find?

Section Two

1. What impact does the drought have on the Worleys?

2. Describe the Watts family and their lifestyle.

3. What excuse does Anna give Bette for not starting a family?

4. Discuss how Ken's arrival impacts the situation at Garra Nalla. What kind of man is he?

5. What is 'the other business' that Ken refers to?

6. Why is the wind becoming an issue? How many days does Anna say the wind has blown?

7. Describe Anna's encounter with the snake.

8. What does Anna tell Stephanie, her sister, in the email?

9. Why does Lohrey include the sections where Luke is reading and Anna is watching the war news (p65-67)? Are these visually distinctive and contrasting images?

10. Where is Gil's son and what is he doing?

11. Discuss Luke and Anna's different views of the city after their return. They see the same things but interpret them differently. Is this part of what being distinctively visual means?

12. Why is Gil opposed to the new forest development?

13. What is your impression of Anna at the conclusion of this section of *Vertigo*?

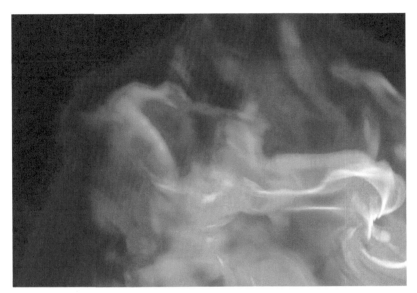

Section Three

1. Why does Anna create the new garden?

2. What is the first description of the bushfire (p91)? Why does it seem to pose little threat?

3. Discuss how Lohrey builds tension before the arrival of the fire.

4. What preparations do the couple make for the coming fire?

5. Why is Anna so worried about the fires?

6. Why do they play tennis with the Watts?

7. Who notices the fire is coming in from the north? Why is this significant for the townspeople?

8. How does the arrival of the fire truck help Luke and Anna?

9. Where are they evacuated to and what happens there?

10. What impact has the fire had on their home?

11. How does Gil see the events?

12. Why does Luke cry?

13. Do you think the novella ends positively, neutrally or negatively about the Worleys and their future? Explain your response with direct reference to the text. Think about the final images.

SETTING

Vertigo is set mainly on the coastline of Australia but there are references to the cityscape that they are escaping. What we learn about setting is that the setting may allow healing and change but you cannot run away from yourself. Garra Nalla does supply some healing but it is the cathartic effect of the fire that is the biggest turning point. Before we analyse this we need to focus on the town itself which is a type of pastiche by Lohrey of the Tasmanian towns that she has experienced, especially Falmouth, her own home town which did experience bushfires. These first hand experiences affected her own psyche and she explores this in the novella.

Garra Nalla is fictional but representational. It is a cluster of eighty odd houses around a 'wild beach' and a lagoon and we can see the significance of that setting by Lohrey spending four pages (11-14) in describing it until we read,

'Perfect, they thought; *just perfect.*' (p14)

Another feature of the setting that Lohrey makes much of is the 'weatherboard homestead from the Federation era' which is also perfect for them as it was 'elemental'. Later we read that Luke settles into this setting but Anna has some doubts about her ability to adapt to the environment. Those sections give great detail on how the setting is used and how Lohrey invokes a variety of techniques to engage the reader and convey her ideas.

To conclude, the 'Australian flavour' of *Vertigo* due to its content and imagery is worth stressing and linking to the Distinctively Visual. Lohrey obviously has affection for the Australian coastal setting. Despite the violence of the bushfire and the destruction it creates we still get a sense of affection for the natural landscape coming through in the writing and also for the wildlife that inhabit that environment.

The descriptions and events show a particular knowledge e.g. the use of casuarinas and the particular references to bird life of that environment as well as the fires. Lohrey creates a setting all can recognise but makes it different in an interesting manner. In part, this is the reason why the novella has been so successful. It is a work about love but the love isn't just confined to characters, the setting makes it all happen and Lohrey's love of the natural landscape shines through.

QUESTIONS ON THE SETTING

1. How does Lohrey portray the city? Do you think there might be some intentional bias on the part of the author? Explain your response with direct reference to *Vertigo*.

2. Why is Garra Nalla 'perfect'?

3. What qualities does the old Federation house have that makes them choose it?

4. Discuss the lagoon. What impact does it have on the narrative?

5. How does the environment seem to enter the town and each character's manner of seeing the world? To respond to this question you could think about the wind and the descriptions of the wind, the tree line and the drought's impact.

6. How does the fire change the landscape? Note here it is not just the descriptions of the burnt areas but also the heat, smoke, dead animals and destroyed buildings. Comment on each of these.

7. What signs of regeneration/rebirth do we see at the end of the novella?

8. How does Lohrey convey the idea that the setting we are in is constantly changing?

9. What images in your mind do the words 'seachange' and 'treechange' evoke? What are their actual meanings?

10. What makes this novel's setting particularly Australian?

CHARACTER ANALYSIS

Luke Worley

Luke is married to Anna and through a major part of the narrative he is affected, as she is, by thoughts arising from the death of their prematurely born son who is known as "the boy". At thirty-four Luke has taken to bird watching as a hobby, perhaps to alleviate the sense of loss. Dissatisfied with his life in the city he begins to feel that life is passing him by and that his optimism is fading 'into something jittery'. Anna agrees to his plan to move into the countryside, partly because she feels the same way. They eventually decide on the coastal hamlet of Garra Nalla where they find a Federation style house that suits them perfectly.

It is here Luke begins to change, slowly finding something that suits him. He becomes handy with things mechanical, a skill he hadn't had previously and slots into the more bucolic lifestyle easily. He is able to merge into the landscape of the town and the surrounds, effectively, aided by his bird-watching. Luke begins to meld into the landscape as if he were a local and this doesn't always sit well with Anna who has plans to return to the city. It appears as if Luke will never do this as his brief trip back doesn't sit well with him. At a restaurant on the final night of his abbreviated stay,

> 'he is prickly and distant, complaining of the noise and making a show of not being able to hear anything said to him.' (p74)

'Nothing pleases him' and Anna is relieved when he goes. Anna and Luke have some issues. She sees him as 'complacent' and as having 'lost all ambition' yet Luke is unmoved and continues without realising her concerns. He is lost in his commune with nature, the local life and the things and people that please him. Luke, at the conclusion of the novella, has come to terms with the loss of his child and we see this in the dream he has after the bushfire has passed and life has some semblance of normality.

> 'somewhere in there, lost to view, is the phantom of the bird on the banksia bough, and he sighs and groans in his sleep, for he'll never see that bird again, and he still doesn't know its name.' (p139)

Luke is a character that sees the visual around him and adapts clearly to his new environment. Certainly the bushfire clarifies and cleanses for him and the seachange that he undergoes affects more than his place of residence. The things he sees change his personality and make him a different person.

Anna Worley

Anna has a different take on the seachange that she and Luke undergo and she follows a different path into the reconciliation with her own life and the death of "the boy". While I feel she is reconciled with his death in the final section she struggles with other factors before coming to this moment when we leave the novella with her and the visually impactful 'ghostly images'. Anna has struggled with life after the death of her child (understandably) and the change she agrees to is partly to overcome this and to change her life which she is generally unhappy with. We read this on page seven and eight,

'Anna appeared to put up little resistance to this migration and they assumed she was concerned about her health. What they couldn't know, because she didn't tell them, was that like her husband she found herself troubled by a falling away of her youthful elan.'

Anna doesn't fit into and adapt to the lifestyle at Narra Garra as easily as Luke who is more 'practical' than she is her but he understands her restlessness. She thinks that she couldn't 'live here all my life' but he ignores her and persists. Later in the novella she finds Luke a 'stranger' and feels,

> 'The world is spinning away from her. Something is dying, something is leaching away from them; some once vivid hue in the inner landscape of her consciousness is beginning to fade.' (p86)

Later, after the fire, she 'frets' for his return and when he does he has had his cathartic experience and cried for "the boy" and they unite. That night she dreams of her lost child and wakes crying, showing her sensitivity to the issue. We see throughout *Vertigo* that she does begin to move on, even thinking about more children. Anna also seems to recover from her asthma to some extent and she certainly becomes more in tune with what is around her.

The Boy

"The boy" is a complex artifice in the novel and I would like you to think about his role in the novel and whether he can be considered a character. It is appropriate here to examine what Lohrey says about her creation,

'I don't want to say too much about him because I'll give away the plot, but he's another dimension of reality. You can read him in several ways. You can read him as a ghost, you can read him as a figment of their imagination. By the time you get to the end of the novella, as you know, you do realise who he is and why he is there. But one of the things I wanted to do was not write a wholly realistic story. I wanted to write a kind of fable, in a way, and so he sits in that as a fabulous figure who may or may not be real.

He relates directly to that sense of disorientation...when you move from the city to the country, as anyone who has made that move can tell you, you very often...all your expectations are confounded. The first thing you often experience is an intense disorientation, hence the title *Vertigo*, which does not relate to a fear of heights, by the way, but to the loss of balance that comes from being in a strange environment and having to find your bearings anew.

So there is this kind of element of the fable where there are certain magical or luminous elements that suggest a more powerful and mysterious reality, which is indeed really what nature is, a more powerful and mysterious reality, than the notion we have of it when we live in the city.'

HTTP://WWW.ABC.NET.AU/RADIONATIONAL/PROGRAMS/BOOKSHOW/AMANDA-LOHREYS-VERTIGO/3179466#TRANSCRIPT

Later in the questions I will ask what you think about this. Lohrey creates a kind of mystical/ephemeral feel to "the boy" and we can see clearly his impact on Luke and Anna.

Gilbert Reilly

Gilbert 'Gil' Reilly is the closest neighbour in Garra Nalla and has a wonderfully extensive knowledge of 'local folklore' and he is fond of a 'natter' or chat. His physical appearance is described,

'tall with a long beaky nose and ginger hair that is thin on top.'
(p25)

Gil becomes a good friend and neighbour, helping them out with advice and practical assistance at times. He has his own family, four children, that don't visit but he doesn't live in the past and this is why Luke and Anna like him. Gil survives the bushfire and they come to think of him as part of why they like the move to the sea. Gil is practical and laconic in a typically Australian way, keeping his own business close and seeing the world with a wry, often ironic, humour. Gil is the kind of character one would expect to find in a small Australian town and in this regard he is nearly stereotypical yet the situation with the son gives him more depth.

The Watts Family

Alan and Bette Watts become friends with the Worleys and they socialise frequently despite the Watts having two children Briony and Zack. The Watts,

> 'belong to that coastal tribe who seem entirely at ease in their sun-ripened bodies and who rarely appear in anything other than shorts or thongs.' (p49)

The Watts are 'energetic and practical' and Luke and Anna seem to warm to them, even sharing confidences along with the barbecues. They have a terrible ordeal during the fire having to cling to the rocks in the bay and worrying about the children. We see Alan's priorities when he tells Luke the details of his 'dread' and Gil responds,

> 'It's all different when your kids are with you.'

The Watts form a counterpoint to the Worley's with their balanced family and easy acceptance of their way of life in Garra Nalla.

Questions on Character

1. Why does Luke want to leave the city?

2. Analyse how Anna's life has changed in the time she has been married before the move to Garra Nalla.

3. Discuss whether you think "the boy" is a character and state reasons for your choice.

4. Does Luke change during his time in Garra Nalla?

5. Describe how Anna comes to resent Luke's behaviour and lifestyle.

6. What effect, if any, does Gil have on the couple?

7. Would you say that Gil is an archetypal Australian country type of character or does he have a larger role than this in the novella?

8. Why might Lohrey include a character such as Rodney Banfield in *Vertigo*?

9. Do you like the Watts family as characters? Analyse the reasons for your decisions about the family and include what role you think they play in the novella.

10. Discuss ONE other character not mentioned in this analysis and state what contribution they make to our understanding and appreciation of *Vertigo*.

THEMATIC CONCERNS

Distinctively Visual

Vertigo needs to be examined within the framework already provided in the section on Experience Through Language and Distinctively Visual as outlined in the Board Requirements section which you should read again before moving on with this. As you know the requirements of this module also require you to examine the images, show how the forms, features and language convey images and how these images are made real or 'visual' by the composer. Of course this isn't the only idea or even the idea Lohrey had when she wrote *Vertigo* but it is the construct by which we will examine the text. An analysis of other related material is needed and you will find a suggested list of at the end of this study guide.

Before we begin I would like to place this idea in its own context and see what the Board would like us to examine when we study Vertigo. The Annotations document suggests several areas worth examining. They are listed below. The full document can be found at:

HTTP://WWW.BOARDOFSTUDIES.NSW.EDU.AU/SYLLABUS_HSC/PDF_DOC/ENGLISH-ANNOTATIONS-2015-20.PDF

NEEDS AND INTERESTS OF STUDENTS

- The power of Lohrey's taut, sensitive descriptive language to evoke images of the natural world and the people who inhabit it, is accessible to all students. It also provides opportunities to extend a wide range of students.
- Students will engage with the fast-moving narrative and its compelling, graphic description of the fire and its aftermath.
- The intriguing title will encourage students to explore its relevance to key ideas in the text.

OPPORTUNITIES FOR CHALLENGING TEACHING AND LEARNING

- The author's use of the haunting, intriguing motif of "the boy" invites students to explore his function in maintaining elements of mystery and suspense.
- The concerns of the text provide scope for the examination of poignant themes of memory and loss, resilience and the search for meaning.
- Students can also consider and evaluate how the ten evocative photographs by Lorraine Biggs enhance the key themes of the novella. (p37)

First, before a purely close analysis, we should generally think about the idea of description in the novella. It is this description that builds images and pictures in the reader's mind. This is how Lohrey conveys not only the narrative, but also the emotions and thoughts of the characters. Later I shall discuss "the boy" and how that picture, a very real picture, manifests itself in the minds of Luke and Anna. A description can be defined as 'a picture in words'. This is an excellent definition for our purpose because this is what Lohrey does for the first page when we read descriptions such as;

> *'There is too much urban jazz in the air, the drone of jets roaring in, the manic whine of sirens or the thumping bass line.' (p3)*

Note here the use of sound to aid in the description. One aspect of good description and a link to your other related text is the use of the five senses to convey information. These senses (sight, sound, taste, touch and smell) are at the core of the novel's descriptions. They help us build visual images of the people, places and events in the novel. Lohrey builds an image of dissatisfaction with the lives of her two main characters. We learn later that "the boy" who is with them at times is a dead child who has scarred them both, but in different ways. "the boy" seems to choose when to appear, not much in the apartment but more when they are free. Lohrey depicts him as if he were real, as he is to Luke and Anna;

> *'Roused from his torpor on the back seat he craned his neck to see out, and wriggling free of his seatbelt scrambled up onto the seat to press his face against the window.' (p11)*

Lohrey even gives him personality, 'he remains loyal to his father' (81) and Anna can even touch and feel him;

> *'his open mouth sighs a warm breath and his eyelids flutter...With her finger she traces the rise of his high forehead, brushing aside the unruly whorls of fair hair...' (p123)*

This is the power of an imaginative vision; his presence is distinctively visual. He is created by Lohrey to add depth to the characters and novel. Also consider the trauma of their loss and how it impacts on how they see the world in general. Does such a loss colour the world and those in it? Certainly an aspect to consider is the narrative line of Gil's "the boy" who is fighting in Afghanistan. This narrative line with "the boy" is only one aspect of the distinctively visual in the text.

Now I wish to explore how Lohrey creates imagery through language around the city and country. It is too easy to state how this seeming paradox would be easy to write about with the bias that the city is bad and the township of Garra Nalla is perfect. Lohrey doesn't do this. She allows us to visualise the distinctive places she pictures and gives us an ambivalence that allows us to decide why the characters act as they do. The city causes Anna's asthma yet when she returns she is pleased to be out of the wind and:

> 'there is much here that is sensual and exciting, and not all of it neon. She loves the lurid metropolitan sunsets...the dark, blackish shapes of the city skyline, the contrast of their sharp-edged silhouettes against a fiery sky, confer on nature an even greater drama.' (p75)

Indeed we can see through these visualisations. We can also see that Luke appreciates the country a little more initially and his bird watching integrated him into nature and the way of life there. Here Luke is happier, 'pointlessly, mindlessly happy' at times just by being in the natural world and a place where he seems to be content. They both find Garra Nalla a place of 'grandeur' and 'just perfect' and the house their 'kingdom'. Examine these early descriptions carefully as they establish much that is relevant in the novel. Think about how you, as the audience, saw these places.

The other aspect of the narrative that deserves attention is the fire which dominates the final third of the book. Luke and Anna have had personal conflict and tension but the fire exacerbates this to an extent then draws them together, especially as "the boy" leaves. The intensity of the experience is described in detail. We see the emotional, as well as physical, impact it has on them and the community in general. Gil's relaxed,

'No-one dead,..so there you are.' (p128)

is typically Australian and relaxed but for others like Gil it was traumatic because of his children. Yet it is the descriptions of the fire, beginning with smoke, that attract the attention of the reader. Lohrey's language engages us and draws us into the scene as if we are with them through the experience. As I have discussed earlier, Lohrey had experienced fires herself and this experience is certainly translated into an understanding of the experience which is shared with us.

The fire itself begins with a 'brown smudge' and builds into,

'A yellow and red fireball ... unravelling from the black underbelly of the smoke cloud. In one incandescent arc it catapults high over the paddocks, across the freeway and down into the bush...' (p113)

The aftermath of nothing but ash upsets Luke so much,

'The wind funnelled anarchy of burning bush, the tidal wave of flame and smoke...'(p130)

The emotion drives him back to the waiting room where he learns of his son's death. The fire ignites emotion and then becomes cathartic. In many ways the fire mirrors their personal experience in that they needed the past to be cleansed away by fire so they could rise again.

Lastly, it is interesting to look at how some emotions are described, using personification.

"That most acidic of beasts, envy, had a fang-hold on her heart."

Contemplate how the words, "acidic, and fang-hold"" add to the image of envy as a beast.

Now I have briefly gone over what Lohrey does in the novella in the context of Distinctively Visual, we next need to explore more of the specific techniques she uses to convey these images.

Questions on Distinctively Visual

1. Define the term Distinctively Visual in your own words.

2. Name TWO images that are distinctively visual which contribute to the audience's understanding and enjoyment of the text.

3. Discuss the difference between the city and the country as exposed in the novella. Do you think it is obvious or is Lohrey more subtle?

4. How do you define the term imaginative vision?

5. Analyse the role of "the boy" in *Vertigo*.

6. Explain the role of the bushfire in the narrative. How does it enhance change or is it just to add conflict to the narrative?

7. While we are focused on the Distinctively Visual as our main idea we also need to think about other concepts. I think the novella is about love, in its various forms. Do you agree with

this thought? Explain your ideas with specific reference to *Vertigo*.

8. Another thought that critics suggest Lohrey alludes to is that of the environment. Do you agree with this suggestion? Explain your response fully and then analyse what she is saying about the environment.

9. In a book that concentrates on the visual how does Lohrey convey emotions such as love?

10. Discuss ONE idea in *Vertigo* that hasn't been discussed here that YOU think is relevant to understanding of the text.

LANGUAGE

Language Techniques

In the previous section the manner in which Lohrey utilises the idea of the Distinctively Visual in her novella and some of the ways in which she does this were explored. Description is one and the following is a specific example of the way Lohrey integrates sensual references into descriptions. Let's look at one now with minor annotations.

'Concealed (sight) beneath a thicket of she-oaks they embraced (touch) on the spiky (touch) ground, enveloped in its pungent (smell) conifer scent and the sound (sound) of the surf, its soft wash (sound) against the rocks below.' (p43)

This example demonstrates how Lohrey uses the senses to enrich her descriptions, build imagery and to allow readers to 'see' that place.

She also uses onomatopoeia to build images eg 'whoomph' and similes such as 'burn like buggery' to communicate specific images through words. You should also note the use of italics throughout the novella as Lohrey uses them in interesting ways. She uses italics in the usual manner to highlight words for emphasis e.g. 'one' (p41) and 'sure' (p125) but also for Latin plant names, extracts from other literary works and titles, as per stylistic conventions. As well as these very specific language techniques that are used to compose highly visual images, we need to examine some of the motifs that she uses to represent complex images.

"the boy" as their dead child is called is more than a recurring image or motif. He is so real to them and to us. He can be considered a character. He does of course represent their past. It is a past they are trying to escape in their sea-change move. Eventually he goes, drifts away, with a wave on the water but I think that the motif that represents "the boy" as a character is the anonymous bird that Luke sees early. The bird is found dead after the fire and Luke is 'distraught' and Anna can't believe he is 'crazily upset about this...this one bird!' (p126) Luke also dreams of the phantom bird as a final sign that "the boy" has gone,

'And somewhere in there, lost to view, is the phantom of the bird on the banksia bough, and he sighs and groans in his sleep, for he'll never see that bird again, and he still doesn't know its name.'
(p139)

Much has been said about "the boy" in his character assessment so I will move into a discussion of another motif, that of the black swans. The black swans are, like the birds in the novella, transcendent of more mundane and mortal, indeed ordinary, considerations. The black swans recur and appear and disappear as they please. In the concluding sections the swans signify life returning to normalcy after the maelstrom of the fires,

'We haven't seen them since the fire...Their nesting grounds around the lagoon were burnt out and we wondered if they were dead, or flown away for good...the swans are back...' (p138)

Personification has also been alluded to earlier in terms of the emotion, envy.

In the author's note at the end of the novella. She states that readers who are familiar with the work of Henry Lawson will recognise intertextual references to two of his short stories, 'The Fire at Ross's Farm' and 'Bushfire'. It is definitely worth exploring these short stories, in order to compare the distincly visual in both and to identify the intertextual links.

Use of Photographs

Before we conclude this section, it is vital to examine the use of the graphics in the novella. These are inserted into the text and form part of the visually distinctive effect that you need to comment on. The quote below explains the use of the photos eloquently and Lohrey explains the purpose of their use,

'Some of the photographs she had. She had photographed the bushfires. So, for example, there's a marvellous photograph in the novella of a fireball. To my knowledge the only photograph of an actual fireball that's in existence, certainly the only one we've ever seen, and we've looked. A quite awe-inspiring image with a thrilling beauty to it.

So she already had some photographs and then I told her about what I was doing, and, as it was still in the draft stage, the kinds of things I would like. I would like some photographs of birds because birds feature quite strongly in the narrative. So she took some more photographs, and then I gave her the manuscript to read in draft. We sat down and chose a long list of the ones we liked. Then we showed them to the publisher. So it was a kind of group effort. We came up with a small collection that we all liked.'

HTTP://WWW.ABC.NET.AU/RADIONATIONAL/PROGRAMS/BOOKSHOW/AMANDA-LOHREYS-VERTIGO/3179466#TRANSCRIPT

It is wise to comment on this aspect of the work in your essay and comment on why they were used and how they add meaning to your reading of *Vertigo*.

Questions on Techniques

1. Give TWO specific examples of the Distinctively Visual and the techniques Lohrey uses to convey that image.

2. Why is it important to create picture images in the reader's mind in a novella such as *Vertigo*. Think about the short story format and the demands of that genre.

3. Find THREE descriptions that use at least four of the five senses. Why might an author such as Lohrey focus on using the senses to engage readers?

4. Comment on the use of one specific language technique used in *Vertigo* and analyse its effect in the novella.

5. Do you find "the boy" more of a motif or a character? Explain your response with direct reference to *Vertigo*.

6. How do birds feature as motifs in Lohrey's work?

7. What particular importance does the unnamed bird have in the narrative?

8. Select ONE description of the bushfire and show, by annotation, how Lohrey creates a picture in the reader's mind.

9. Describe one image in the narrative that particularly struck you and why it impacted you.

10. Why has Lohrey combined with an artist to include graphics in the novella? What do they add to the narrative and the reader's understanding?

11. If you had the opportunity to add a new graphic to *Vertigo* what would it be and where in the novella would you place it?

THE ESSAY

The essay has been the subject of numerous texts and you should have the basic form well in hand. As teachers, the point we would emphasise would be to link the paragraphs both to each other and back to your argument (which should directly respond to the question). Of course ensure your argument is logical and sustained.

Make sure you use specific examples and that your quotes are accurate. To ensure that you respond to the question make sure you plan carefully and are sure what relevant point each paragraph is making. It is solid technique to actually 'tie up' each point by explicitly coming back to the question.

When composing an essay the basic conventions of the form are:

> - State your argument, outline the points to be addressed and perhaps have a brief definition.

↓

> A solid structure for each paragraph is:
> - Topic sentence (the main idea and its link to the previous paragraph/ argument)
> - Explanation / discussion of the point including links between texts if applicable.
> - Detailed evidence (Close textual reference- quotes, incidents and technique discussion.)
> - Tie up by restating the point's relevance to argument / question

↓

> - Summary of points
> - Final sentence that restates your argument

As well as this basic structure you will need to focus on:

Audience – for the essay the audience must be considered formal unless specifically stated otherwise. Therefore your language must reflect the audience. This gives you the opportunity to use the jargon and vocabulary that you have learnt in English. For the audience ensure your introduction is clear and has impact. Avoid slang or colloquial language including contractions (like doesn't, eg, etc).

Purpose – the purpose of the essay is to answer the question given. The examiner evaluates how well you can make an argument and understand the module's issues and its text(s). An essay is solidly structured so its composer can analyse ideas. This is where you earn marks. It does not retell the story or state the obvious. Because the purpose is to respond to the set question, rewriting an essay you may have scored well in previously, will not work in a new situation with a new question.

Communication – Take a few minutes to plan the essay. If you rush into your answer it is almost certain you will not make the most of the brief 40 minutes to show all you know about the question. More likely you will include irrelevant details that do not gain you marks but waste your precious time. Remember an essay is formal so **do not** do the following: story-tell, list and number points, misquote, use slang or colloquial language, be vague, use non sentences or fail to address the question.

HSC STYLE ESSAY QUESTION– *VERTIGO*

'If places and times are portrayed clearly in texts, then the experiences of characters also come to life for responders'.

Evaluate how effectively the Distinctively Visual lens captures places, times, people and experiences in your set text and at least one related text.

Read the question carefully and then examine the essay outline on the following pages. Try to develop your essay along these lines.

You should also develop strategies to answer questions that are not essay based. A list of these different types of question is given at the back, along with additional essay style questions. Look at these. You should be familiar with most of the text types. Try to practise as many questions as you can, both essay style and non-essay style, to develop your writing skills.

A few hints for the question above-

- Do not ignore the quotation altogether. It is important you take note of the ideas and check your response does address them.
- Take care you use the number of texts the examiner asks for. There is no value in writing on more and you will **definitely** be penalised for writing on less.
- You MUST have quotations and textual references that show you have a good knowledge and understanding of your prescribed AND other text.
- Your response must look at BOTH **WHAT** the texts have taught you about the importance of exploring interactions AND **HOW** the composer represented those ideas.

PLAN: Don't even think about starting without one!

Introduce... The texts you are using in the response. Your thesis or argument. Explanation of the Distinctively Visual and its portrayal in the texts with reference to question. • Argument: *Vertigo* and one ORT is able to portray places, times, people and experiences effectively through techniques that convey clear images to the responder	You need to let the marker know what texts you are discussing. You can start with a definition but it could come in the first paragraph of the body. You MUST state your argument in response to the question and the points you will cover as part of it. Don't wait until the end of the response to give it!

↓

Idea 1- Places are times are conveyed clearly using techniques relevant to text type. • explain the idea • where and how shown in *Vertigo* and one related text **Idea 2- People and experiences come alive due to clear portrayal of contextual aspects.** • explain the idea • where and how shown in *Vertigo* and one related text • Explain techniques i.e. how.	You can use the things you have learned to organise the essay. For each one you say where you saw this in your prescribed text and where in the other text. Two ideas are usually enough as you can explore them in detail.

↓

• Summary of two key ideas • Final sentence that restates your argument. Do not raise new points and link points back to the question.	Make sure your conclusion restates your argument. It does not have to be too long.

DISTINCTIVELY VISUAL: OTHER RELATED TEXTS

Film

Sliding Doors Dir. Peter Howitt

This 1998 film has very visual ideas also highlighting the theme of chance and fate. The narrative primarily revolves around how one incident can change the timing of your life and consequently the rest of your life. In this case, the one incident was a woman missing or catching a train. When she caught the train, she came home early to find her partner in bed with another woman. Consequently, she ends a long term relationship and begins a life as an independent woman who finds the challenges of her new found life enable her to find a better life. However, when she misses the train, the woman is out of her house before she can catch her partner cheating on her. Her life continues as normal and she is miserable.

In the end, the concept of fate is reiterated when her life does end up very similar, regardless of which path was selected. Techniques that are used excellently in this film are editing and camera angles.

Forbidden Planet Dir. Fred M Wilcox

This 1956 classic was nominated in two categories for visual effects and special effects for an Academy Award. This film is based on Shakespeare's *The Tempest* and has the wonderful Robby the Robot, a cinematic legend. The visuals are highly distinctive.

While the film is old it is a basis for many films that followed. Highly recommended.

Star Wars: Episode IV - A New Hope Dir. George Lucas

This is a wonderful, fantastical film and distinctively visual in so many ways. A forerunner of special effects in 1977 it won Academy Awards in art direction, set decoration, special effects, visual effects, costume and editing. There are many features in this film to discuss and relate back to your text.

The Birds Dir. Alfred Hitchcock

This 1963 film is only one of two horror films by the great director, the other being *Psycho*. This film won best effects and visual effects for its stunning portrayal of bird attacks in the seaside hamlet of Bodega Bay.

Lucy Dir. Luc Besson

This 2014 movie featuring Scarlett Johannson and directed by Frenchman Luc Besson is visually stunning. As reluctant drug mule Lucy ingests a new drug and the world opens up to her. She and the audience, see the world in a new way as her brain operates at full capacity. Awesome visuals and intercut footage combine with CGI effects to give us a modern, visually distinctive film.

Photography

Below is a short list of photographs that have features which are distinctively visual to give you an idea of what to look for. When commenting on these you need to state what is the distinctively visual features but also what the purpose of the photograph might be that the features illustrate.

- Dieter Appelt - *Liberation of the Fingers* (1979)
- Nan Goldin - *Rise and Monty on the Lounge Chair* (1988)
- Joyce Neimanas - *Face Lift* (1993)
- Bea Nettles - *Floating Fish Fantasy* (1976)
- Zee Berman - *Inversions* (1991)

Another method of approaching this is to pick a photographer that appeals to you and examine their body of work, citing two or three photos that appeal to you. Some examples might be Robert Maplethorpe, Max Dupan, Nick Utz and Anna-Lou 'Annie' Leibovitz.

Art

Another source of visually distinctive other related material is art. Of course art may not have language features that you may want but it certainly does have plenty of visuals that you can discuss and link to the artist's thematic concerns and purpose. Of course any art is subjective so select an artist that you like and one who has something that is truly visually distinctive or new for that period.

- Odilon Redon - *la Mort D'Ophelie* (1900-05)
- Jan Vermeer - *Girl with a Pearl Earring* (1665-6)
- Edward Hopper - *Chop Suey* (1929)
- Salvador Dali - *Le Sommeil* (1937)
- Willem De Kooning - *Woman* (1950)
- Ian Abdulla - *Sowing Seeds at Night* (1990)

Again you can certainly choose an artist and focus on a specific style or school. Artists like Andy Warhol are modern and easily accessible.

Picture Books

These are by nature extremely visually distinctive and many also have a written narrative that accompanies the graphic images which allows for further explanation of the images and their purpose. Some examples are given below but you can find many in your school and local library. When analysing these, be use to use the language of visual literacy.

The Wind Blew - Pat Hutchins

This is a more traditional picture book with limited text and a fun but conservative drawing style for modern times. It provides an effective contrast with your set text. It has a distinctive style.

Angry Arthur - Hiawyn Oram and Satoshi Kitamura

Modern and brightly distinctive graphics illustrate the story of angry Arthur whose angry thoughts cause an 'universequake' which is quite a thing as you can imagine. It is a British book but relevant in that it questions anger in our lives.

Cinnamon, Mint and Mothballs - Ake Sogabe and Ruth Tiller

This text is distinctive in that it uses cut paper illustrations and the story is in Haiku form. It presents a very intriguing visit to Grandmother's house. The illustrations are extremely visually distinctive.

The Clown of God - Tomie dePaola

This is the story, retold, of the little juggler, which is a French tale. The illustrations are colourful in part, sepia toned in part and closely follow the narrative which is more language intense than many picture books.

Poetry

Poets use words to create distinctively visual imagery in the audience's mind. Here you could look for descriptive poems about nature and natural elements that the poet has shown in a new way through words. Poets always are trying to convey an idea or theme and the words have a purpose so they link well with the set text. Consider the work of some of the Romantic poets whose theme is nature. Coleridge's 'This Lime Tree Bower my Prison' and Wordsworth's 'Daffodils' are worth exploring. Likewise, Browning's 'My Last Duchess' paints a strong picture of the speaker in this dramatic monologue.

Images

Google "web" and "images" can give you some great material. You could enter in various key words that relate to the main ideas of the text you are studying. Such key words could include "fire", "destiny" and "ghostlike". You have already seen some images in the beginning of this study guide. Some samples follow to give you an idea. be sure to acknowledge your sources in essays or other responses.

OTHER RESOURCES FOR RELATED MATERIAL

Prior to 2015 the following texts were on the HSC Standard Prescriptions list for Module A: Experience through Language, Elective 2: Distinctively Visual-

- Poetry by Douglas Stewart

- *Run Lola Run*, a film by Tom Tykwer

- *Seachange* episodes, a media text

- and, for prose fiction, Peter Goldsworthy's novel *Maestro*.

- Three of these texts are still available in the Top Notes series. Remember that they have been written with this Module and Elective specifically in mind. While these texts are no longer core or prescribed texts for this elective, they can be used as related material. Look up the Five Senses website - www.fivesenseseducation.com.au to order online. Even if you are studying a different film or prose fiction or set of poems, the material and approach outlined in the guides is still helpful. In this instance, you are advised not to focus on *Maestro* as it is Prose Fiction as is your prescribed text, *Vertigo*. You are best advised to select other text types for your related material.

- Top Notes -Selected Poems: Douglas Stewart by Yanis Garrett

- Top Notes -Prose Fiction: *Maestro* by William Burden and Giuliana Gorman

- Top Notes - Film: *Run Lola Run* by Tom Tykwer's

OTHER TYPES OF RESPONSES

It is crucial students realise that their responses in the examination, class and assessment tasks will not necessarily be essays. This page is designed to give guidance with the different types of responses which are possible.

The response types covered in the examination may include any of the following:

- Feature Article
- Journal/Diary entry
- Letter/ email
- Point of View
- Radio Interview
- Report
- Speech
- Television Interview
- Website
- Writing in a Role

OTHER RESPONSES TO PRACTISE

Class style question

1. An expert on fiction is writing a feature article for Reader's World magazine to celebrate Amanda Lohrey's novella. The article argues that Lohrey's novella has distinctively visual features that make it a valuable text in Australian literature

Examination style question

1. An expert on writing is submitting a feature article for Reader's World magazine to celebrate the importance of place. The article argues that distinctively visual features of texts, help to convey not only place but time and events.

    Write the article referring to specific elements of the novella.

Class style essay question

2. 'Lohrey's work is more about images than events.'

    To what extent do you agree with this statement? In your answer refer specifically to at least TWO incidents and/or characters in the novella.

Examination style essay question

3. 'Texts in the Distinctively Visual Elective are focussed more on images than events.'

    To what extent do you agree with this statement? In your answer refer closely to your prescribed text and one other.

The previous examples show you the importance of close study of text in preparation for examination style questions. The following are questions intended for class use. Re write Q 4,5 and 6 in a style more suited to the HSC examination. Then select two questions and write your response in forty minutes for each.

4. 'Lohrey is celebrated for the effective visual techniques she uses to represent vibrant images of Australian life.'

    How does Lohrey create such vibrant images? In your answer refer specifically to the text.

5. Imagine you are Amanda Lohrey. Write a series of journal entries where you reflect on how you have used visual images to make your novella, *Vertigo,* more engaging.

    In your answer, refer specifically to *Vertigo*.

6. Two HSC students studying Distinctively Visual are discussing how composers shape meaning through the distinctively visual. Write their conversation where they discuss Lohrey's *Vertigo* and a related text in detail. They speak about their responses to the ideas and techniques of two texts.

7. Create a visual representation of your response to Lohrey's use of the distinctively visual. Your representation should include relevant graphics, key words and phrases and anything else you feel communicates your response.

    When complete, write a reflection statement where you explain your composition and how it represents the ideas of the elective.